MOTHER CHAT

MOTHER CHAT

Judy Gardiner

Illustrations

Tony Hatt

FREDERICK MULLER LIMITED
LONDON

First published in Great Britain in 1979
by Frederick Muller Limited, London NW2 6LE

British Library Cataloguing in Publication Data

Gardiner, Judy
  Mother chat.
  1. Mothers
  I. Title
  301.42'7   HQ759

  ISBN 0-584-10355-7

Typeset by Texet, Leighton Buzzard, Bedfordshire.

Printed in Great Britain by Billing & Sons Ltd.,
Guildford, London and Worcester.

Contents

Dedicated to all mothers in general,
and ours in particular

Preface

When I was born my mother woke up from the chloroform and said 'What have I got?'

'A baby!' cried the nurse, who was young and easily surprised. 'Damn,' said my mother, and went back to sleep.

I can't blame her. Nine months is a long time to spend on any sort of *oeuvre* — I have it on authority that it only takes three hours to make a whole Ford Fiesta and it's no use arguing that Fords are specially tooled up for the job; so are mothers.

But there's a lot more to it than that, of course. The making of a baby and the making of a mother (for they make one another simultaneously, apart from the initial kick-start), is a far more nervy, titchy tetchy business; more like composing a sonata, except that you can't see any of the notes you've written until the thing's complete. You can't even hear it, except inside your head.

With a baby all you can do is to feel, and to imagine, and perhaps be given a brief glimpse of the full-term X-ray, and by the time you've lumbered from January to October you could well have gone off the boil about the whole idea.

But the fortitude of mothers never ceases to amaze me. Even when the nine months are up they're faced with eighteen months of nappy-washing, five years before it goes to school and anything up to another fifteen before it leaves home and learns to shift for itself. It's a long, long haul, and during the course of it the mother will also have to adjust herself to the fact that she is never, after all, going to be Home Secretary or a member of the Royal Shakespeare. She's not even going to make Spanish for Beginners at the local Tech. unless someone volunteers to wash up after supper, and the only new status she's ever likely to acquire is that of mother-in-law. And after that, grandmother.

I believe in the Liberated Woman, but find my affection reserved for the girl struggling to do her week's shopping in the supermarket in defiance of a screaming baby and a couple of small children who insist on building castles with tins of baked beans. She looks tired and down at heel, but when you catch her eye she gives you a sudden rueful, humorous grin that warms you all the way home.

Coming back to my own mother, I once asked her why she was so disconcerted at being told she'd had a baby. What else was she expecting?

'Your father promised me a yacht,' she said.

1

In the Beginning

If all the world's mothers were laid end to end simultaneously there would be no room left to park a car, which would be nice. Except that they'd soon get round to sticking parking tickets on mothers, because they've got to raise the money from somewhere.

Mothers come in assorted sizes, shapes and colours and the age at which mothers can actually become mothers ranges roughly between twelve and fifty-five, although it must be emphasised that both figures quoted are extreme and are therefore (in relation to pregnancy) apt to give rise to consternation within the family circle.

Mothers can be happy or sad, lethargic or sprightly, resourceful or dim; they can be ravishingly beautiful or painfully plain — the average, I suppose, is somewhere in between — but despite their marvellous and heartwarming diversity, they all have one thing in common. They are all women.

So far. For men have been dying to get in on the act for over a thousand years, but up until now have had to content themselves with writing books telling women that they (the women) could do it a whole lot better if only they would follow their (the men's) advice. The first book on obstetrics, incidentally, was written in 1513 by a man called Eucharius Roslin at the invitation of his patroness, the Duchess of Brunswick. It was something of a medieval best-seller with its references to fumigation by doves' dung etc. and was published in England under the all-embracing title of *The Byrthe of Mankynde.*

And most people think that the test-tube baby is something new, but it isn't. A mad cleric in Poland is supposed to have bred a whole live baby in a bottle as far back as 1602 and it would have been a triumphant success if only he hadn't overlooked one thing. By the time it was ready to be born it was too big to come out of the bottle. Typically, he blamed this on the baby, who didn't particularly want to come out of the bottle anyway, and I believe that the whole silly business ended in stalemate.

The first officially recognised mother was Eve. She had two sons called Cain and Abel, and then a third one called Seth, who was born when Adam was 130. Genesis doesn't tell us how old Eve was; in fact, having recorded the bit about the apple, treatment of her is cursory in the extreme. Milton admits that she was beautiful, but recounts the story of her temptation and subsequent downfall with a lascivious delight that borders on the pornographic, what with Satan being *Squat like a toad . . . assaying by his Devilish art to reach the Organs of her Fancie . . .* etc. etc.

I like to imagine Eve as she appears in the Mabuse painting that once belonged to Henry the Eighth; standing close to Adam she looks very young and waif-like and has a decidedly apprehensive expression in her eyes. (As well she might, for it must have been a disconcerting experience having the world's first baby — looking down at the wet squalling thing and wondering what the dickens it was *for* . . .)

I wish I could think that the boys were nice to her when they grew up, but what with Cain slaying Abel and then Seth committing incest with her (for how else could he have come by Enos?) I fear she must have known a lot of heartache. Still, things were different in those days.

And talking of things being different reminds me that one of the great myths of my youth concerned the ease with which black mothers gave birth, compared to their white sisters. *All they do is drop out behind a bush, have it quite painlessly, then wash it in the river and carry on*, my elders were fond of saying, so I had this picture of black ladies padding in endless procession through the jungle and only pausing once in every nine months for a fleeting act of parturition. To begin with I was merely curious to know where they were all going, then it struck me as suspiciously convenient that there should always be a river nearby. It was only in my truculent teens that I challenged the assumption that black women have babies with any less pain than white ones, although to be fair I do seem to remember the remark being made in tones of admiring awe rather than condescension.

Now that I'm elderly and serene however, I've come to the conclusion that if any woman, whatever her colour or creed, gives birth behind a bush, it's perfectly okay so long as that's the way she wants it. It's only abominable if she has no alternative.

It's odd to think of the strength and variety of human emotion engendered by pregnancy and childbirth; as a subject it must have had more fantasy and superstition draped about it than any other, apart from death.

Women wishing to become pregnant have been known to embrace trees, throw live pigs into the sacred vaults of Demeter, suck pebbles, clasp red cotton dolls to their bosoms, and in the town of Qua, which was near to Old Calabar, they had a thing about munching coconuts from a special palm tree which grew there.

And having become pregnant by the aid of what-or-whoever, they in turn became the object of even more bigoted goings-on. The theory that both menstruating and pregnant women alike are unsavoury, unclean and best left to their own devices, was widely held all over the world. From Tahiti to Alaska, the poor expectant mother was shunted off into miserable seclusion — in some places men believed that even the shadow of a pregnant woman falling across them could cause them to sicken and die — and on the island of Kadiak she was considered not only too unclean to handle food herself, but even to be fed by anyone else, so her meals were passed to her on what amounted to sort of elongated chop sticks. A messy business.

Yet in spite of the squeamish dislike she so frequently aroused, the pregnant woman (or perhaps one should say the *idea* of a pregnant woman), has also been associated with magical powers of a wholly benevolent kind. Everywhere since the human race began she has been closely linked with harvest, i.e. Corn Mothers, Maize Mothers, Barley Mothers, Rye Mothers, Flax Mothers etc., and in all of them exemplifying what Frazer describes as *The Great Mother-Goddess, the personification of all the reproductive energies of nature.* I wonder if it would help

4

solve the present day energy problem if we had a Fuel Mother?

In Bavaria in the fourteenth century it was believed that offering the first fruit from your tree to a pregnant woman would ensure a bumper crop the following year; in Upper Silesia they believed that the touch of a pregnant woman's hand on the hide of any farm animal in a similar condition would bring about the safe delivery of a healthy offspring, and the sight of an impregnated Mexican lady was supposed to (i) prevent bees from swarming and (ii) promote an improved rate of growth in men's beards.

And if you're the kind of person who mourns the fading of such harmless and rather charming superstitions — take heart. Only last summer I was leaning over the cottage gate of a retired farm worker in Suffolk, admiring his bed of *lilium regale* and asking him what fertilizer he used.

'Fertilizer?' he said, 'they don't git no fertilizer, mate. Me married daughter's six months gorn and I just gits her to piddle under 'em.'

To be accurate, mothers are only mothers from the moment when their babies are born. Prior to that they are merely expectant mothers, mothers-to-be, ladies-in-waiting, or whatever other euphemism you may prefer. Some of them will have managed the entire course of pregnancy with the light of happy anticipation gleaming unabated in their eyes, while others, who started off gladly enough, will have become bored to tears by the fourth month and by the seventh no longer care whether they give birth to a human being or a litter of white mice.

Which reminds me of poor . . . *Dorothie, an Italian (who) had twentie children at two births; at the first nine, at the second eleven, and shee was so big that shee was forced to bear up her bellie, which laie upon her knees, with a broad and large scarfe tied about her neck . . .*

But despite the long boredom of morning sickness, heartburn, varicose veins, swollen ankles, wind, piles, and a predilection for eating soused herrings around 3 a.m., and despite the panic, pain and awful indignity attendant upon the drama's final act — it has recently been established that ninety-eight per cent of mothers, both animal and human, experience this sudden amazing upsurge of love for the little creature that has just come out of them. It starts at the first moment they set eyes on it, and although psychiatrists may be correct in assuming that the abrupt cessation of pain has something to do with it, it must still be one of the strongest, most primitive and most passionate forms of love known to the living world. It's a love that takes us back almost to the birth of time itself, and only a fool would seek to meddle with it.

Yet I'll never forget my glimpse of the girl who formed part of the two per cent for whom the Great Upsurge doesn't happen. And the terrible thing is that she knew it wasn't going to happen, but no one would believe her.

She came into the maternity hospital, very young and very, very pale, and she gave birth to her baby quietly and without fuss. It was her fifth in six years, and the whisper went round the ward that she had asked the doctor more than once whether she could have this pregnancy terminated. She couldn't cope. He told her that there was no reason why she shouldn't have another baby. She said they couldn't afford it. He told her that they should have thought of that before, and that she should go away and pull her socks up. While she was in labour she told the nurses that she wasn't going to take the baby home. They smiled and jollied her along: 'Ah, but wait until you see it! (Push dear — now push hard . . .)' When it arrived she

7

turned her head away. She refused to feed it.

Her husband came to visit her in the evenings, a small man, also very young, with pale eyes set in a pointed face. He used to sit by her bed and hold her hand while she lay staring at the ceiling. After the third day the nurses stopped taking the baby to her, in the hope that deprivation would do the trick. It didn't. She betrayed not the slightest interest in its welfare.

When the day came for her to go home, the atmosphere in the ward was strained. The gynaecologist came specially to talk to her, and then a lady in a white overall and brogues who said, 'Well after all, it isn't as if you're not *married* . . .' The girl didn't say anything, and when her husband arrived in the afternoon with the small shabby case containing her things, she took it along to the bathroom and got dressed. While she was gone the Ward Sister came along with the baby and laid it on the bed with a smile and a knowing wink at the husband. He looked very pale and out of his depth. One of the mothers further down the ward suddenly burst into tears.

The girl came back and she looked like death; marble pale and worn thin as a beanpole. She packed the few odds and ends from her locker into the case, closed it and began to walk away. The Sister picked up the baby, tightly rolled in its shawl, and ran after her. She tried to put it in the girl's arms. She tried to talk to her, gently, urgently, coaxingly, any way she could think of to break through the ice. It made no difference. The girl just kept on walking. The Sister changed tactics and thrust the baby at the father, who looked at it hopelessly, shook his head, tried to smile and then bolted after his wife. The Sister was left holding the baby like a bunch of flowers that nobody wanted to buy.

This happened in 1948, back in the days before women were considered capable of judging whether or not they wanted to bear another child. I watched it all from the bed opposite, holding the curled fingers of my own little daughter in my hand.

There used to be an old wife's tale to the effect that babies prefer to arrive at night so that no one will see their souls slipping into their bodies. It's a nice idea, and could perhaps account for those prolonged fits of inconsolable weeping in which newborn babies sometimes indulge; someone up there has fluffed it, and they've been given the wrong soul by mistake.

And while we're on the subject of old wives, it's all very well to throw up our hands in horror at the thought of the dirty, clumsy and ignorant old Sairey Gamps who attended women in childbirth, but until comparatively recently there was no alternative. Physicians seemed to go through a prolonged period of not wanting to know, and clung to the convenient biblical notion that women should suffer the pangs of labour unassuaged. (*For I have heard a voice as of a woman in travail and the anguish as of her that bringeth forth her first child, the voice of the daughter of Zion, that bewaileth herself, that spreadeth her hands crying Woe is me now! . . .*)

In the Middle Ages the only man who might be prevailed upon to assist at an unusually difficult birth was either a barber or a pig-gelder, and if he had nothing better to do the local executioner might occasionally be persuaded to have a bash at a rough and ready Caesarean section when all else had failed; an ordeal which the poor mother rarely survived.

Yet the rigours of those days pale into insignificance

compared to the horrors of the great lying-in hospitals and charity hospitals of later years, where sufferers from infectious diseases were herded together with women in labour and patients undergoing surgery. In the notorious Hotel de Dieu in Paris the over-crowding was so extreme that it was commonplace for five women to share one bed in the lying-in ward, and of those who survived delivery, twenty per cent succumbed to puerperal fever.

Puerperal or childbirth fever spread throughout Europe in a series of huge epidemics, and in Lombardy in 1773 the toll of life was so terrible that for one entire year not one woman is supposed to have survived giving birth. The death rate only began to fall when Semmelweis and Lister introduced antiseptics during the latter half of the nineteenth century.

And another man whom mothers have cause to bless is the estimable Doctor Simpson, professor of obstetrics at Glasgow University, who first administered chloroform to lessen the torment of a lady in labour in the year 1847. They were both so pleased with the result that the doctor published a paper giving details of his success, but instead of acclaim, all he received was vilification, particularly from the clergy. Chloro-form was a decoy of Satan, they said, and the weight of their condemnation might have crushed a lesser man. But not Doctor Simpson, and his subsequent paper *Answers to the Religious Objection Against the Employment of Anaesthetic Agents in Midwifery and Surgery* was a wonderful blend of logic, erudition and humorous good sense, which he concluded with a quotation from Genesis Chapter 2 Verse 21, in which . . . *the Lord God caused a deep sleep to fall upon Adam, and he slept; and He took one of his ribs, and closed up the flesh instead thereof* . . . and it

11

was this merciful action on the part of the Almighty in causing Adam to fall asleep, argued Doctor Simpson, which surely proved beyond all doubt that the first surgical operation ever performed was accompanied by anaesthesia.

Objections rumbled on nevertheless, and in England it took Queen Victoria's sensible decision to avail herself of chloroform during the birth of her seventh child to bring respectability to the doctor's theory that there's no point in suffering for its own sake.

He died Sir James Simpson Bart. in 1870, and in Glasgow all the shops closed on the day of his funeral.

Over the years mothers have given birth in some pretty strange places, when you come to think of it. Behind bushes, in taxis, in aeroplanes, in trunks (according to Judy Garland), and spare a thought for the country tweeny called Eliza Gibbons who *bore a bastard behind the stillroom door, wrapped it in a dish clout and laid it before one Giles Appleyard, coachman and groom serving at the same establishment.* What became of it after that is not recorded, but I daresay it grew up to take its humble place in the ordered scheme of things.

In my day of course, privacy was all, and no woman worth her salt would have dreamed of being seen by anyone, other than the necessary technicians, until she was tidied up and ready to greet the world in her new role of Little Mother Mild among the grapes and tuberoses. But I gather that nowadays fathers (suitably attired in white masks and gowns) are invariably present at the birth of their children, an idea which strikes me as a bit creepy, although I've been assured by countless young parents that this isn't the case at all. In fact the young chap who's illustrating this book was present at the birth of his own son, so perhaps he has a viable comment to offer:

Well yes, I think I see what he means. And somehow I think that he's just had the last word in this chapter.

2

Other Girls' Mothers

'This may hurt a little, but only temporarily,' I said to Brenda Pommerol and stuck a golf tee up her behind. At that moment the door opened and her mother stood there, and looking across at her scarlet, scandalised face, instinct told me that I had just made an enemy for life.

'What in heaven's name are you doing?' she demanded when the power of speech returned.

With a makeshift nurse's cap pressed low down over my eyes and with Brenda's knickers round her ankles, there seemed little point in saying *Nothing, Mrs. Pommerol.*

'We were playing suppositories,' I said, 'until we were interrupted.'

She told me that I was never to play with Brenda again. That I was never even to speak to her. This didn't upset me very much because Brenda was a lumpish, rather uninteresting child and we only visited one another's houses because they were conveniently placed on the same side of the road.

What did interest me was her mother's hatred; it

14

sparkled in her eyes and snapped at the corners of her mouth and made it quite impossible to explain that it takes two people to play suppositories. So I went home, and Mrs. Pommerol must have instilled the fear of God into her daughter because she never once spoke to me again, not even at the little Dame School we both attended, and on Parents' Day Mrs. P. rewarded my mother's innocent 'Good-afternoon' with a frigid stare.

I've since discovered that most mothers are capable of implacable hatred towards other mothers' children; it's as if the fierce love they feel for their own offspring needs some kind of counterbalance to keep them emotionally upright, and I've certainly been hated by a variety of mothers in my time — not necessarily for bad behaviour, but simply because I wasn't theirs. Whether staying as a house guest or merely as a visitor for tea, I could invariably sense the chill criticism behind the bright smile and the veiled hostility beneath the invitation to have another scone. I think that mothers who have only one child are the most prone to Other Child Abhorrence, for at the other end of the scale I remember a schoolmaster's family of seven vociferous children where the mother was absent-mindedly inclined to include me in the ritual of bath and supper, although I had only called round to swap a couple of bird's eggs . . .

But sometimes when insomnia nags, my thoughts roam back to the past and I find myself wondering what became of Brenda Pommerol; and I can't help thinking how extraordinary it would be if the golf tee is still where I placed it on that golden afternoon when we were both eight.

When I was young schoolgirls were always very interested in one another's mothers. Above the age of ten most of them had rather piercing powers of appraisal and generally speaking were not slow to remark on anything that might strike them as even slightly untoward. Hence:

Milly's mother wears stockings with clocks.

Cynthia Farr's mother says Greta Garbo's a man.

16

Patsy Jenkins' mother lets her read medical books.

Not infrequently, casual gossip rose to a level of high scandalmongering, as in the case of Pam Benton's mother, who was seen to crunch brazil nut toffee all through Speech Day, and then there was a girl called Honoria Somebody-or-Other who enjoyed a dangerous reputation founded on the rumour that her mother drank créme de menthe for breakfast.

Considering that I was one for a little vicarious glory of my own, I once put out a rumour that my mother was one of the Begums of Oude; a rash move, considering that apart from being attracted by the name, I knew nothing about either Begums or Oude. The statement was received in hostile silence.

'So what does that make you?' someone finally demanded, and I recognised that their ignorance was as great as mine.

'A sort of Honourable,' I said. 'But of course we don't use our titles in England.'

Naturally, it was only a couple of days before someone looked up the appropriate reference in the school library, but for some reason the resulting ignominy merely drove me to further recklessness. I told them that I'd made up the bit about the Begums of Oude because the real truth was too painfully embarrassing to talk about; the real fact was that my mother had a wooden leg.

Not only was this received with less hostility, it became a subject of considerable ghoulish interest, until once again I got carried away and told them that she had lost her own leg in 1915, being the only woman to take part in the Battle of Neuve Chapelle, for which she had won both the V.C. and an emotional embrace from King George the Fifth.

They didn't believe me, and sick with self-pity I

asked God if he couldn't do something to make my mother appear more interesting in the eyes of my friends. Strangely enough the request was answered on my twelfth birthday, when purely at my mother's insistence I invited several girls home to tea.

We lived in a rambling ground-floor flat at the time and I saw their busy eyes assessing the dried poppy heads painted gold, the Spanish shawl draped over the grand piano and the two woodcuts of naked women in their oval frames. My mother poured tea and passed round birthday cake with great vivacity and when the meal was finished she suddenly pushed back the table and said: 'Come on, let's give them *Blue Sky* —'

Conscious of a reluctance to mix school and home I at first declined, but my mother's enthusiasm was of the sort never to be resisted. So she and I lined up over by the door, and with her hands on my gym-slipped waist we pranced in step into the centre of the room and before the incredulous eyes of my school-friends began to sing loudly and with great animation:

There's a blue sky o-ver Florida
There's a sun high o-ver Florida —
Where the scent of flowers per-fumes the air
For it's always summer o-ver there —

and on the appropriate beat we executed a high kick, first to the left and then to the right. The floor shook and the seeds rattled in the dried poppy heads, for my mother tipped the scales at about fifteen stone, her glands having reputedly gone wrong after I was born.

There's a girl who waits in Florida
And I love each go-lden curl —
The wedding bells will soon be ringing and you'll
hear those darkies singing
When I marry my Florida girl — HI! —

We then went in to a vigorous tap dance which made the two naked women leap in their frames, repeated the last four lines (rather more breathlessly) then swept down in a low obeisance before the audience.

'*The Sunshine Girl*,' panted my mother. 'Got the bird in Grimsby and rave notices in Yarmouth. Dear old Randolph Sutton in the lead —'

'Do you mean to say,' said the first of my school friends to gather herself together, 'that you're actually on the stage?'

'Was,' said my mother. Then falling on her knees in front of them clasped her plump hands together and sang in an anguished, but extremely sweet voice: '*Spare Oh spare him, I implore you! Humbly here I kneel before you! Dungeons dark for him I dread; wo-on't you punish me-e-e instead? . . .*' Then turning to me with tears in her eyes and a sob in her voice: '*Oh Baldassare . . . Oh Baldassare . . . I never meant . . . I never planned . . .*'

'*That's all right, Teresa*,' I intoned gruffly. '*I understand . . .*' And leaning forward touched her bowed head with a kindly hand.

Neither of us saw anything in the least funny about my taking the part of the brigand hero from *The Maid of the Mountains*. I had been doing it since I was about four. I had, in fact, been taking whatever part was required of me, and knew the score backwards. I also knew long passages from *Jack-and-the-Beanstalk, Aladdin*, and an ill-fated musical called *Dear Love* in which my mother understudied Vera Pearce, another large lady who was always knocking Sidney Howard over with her bust. Upon my friends' request my mother gave a demonstration of the art of knocking people over with one's bust; she knocked me over, rushing at me like a playful express train, and my friends were so captivated that she knocked them over too, until the floor was littered with recumbent school-girls who couldn't get up for giggling. She then gave them a lesson in the soft-shoe-shuffle, and when they had mastered a few steps, drew black soot moustaches under their noses to lend a bit of atmosphere.

We then returned to *The Maid of the Mountains*:

I captured this brooch
From a girl on a coach (flourish, flourish)
And her look of reproach quite upset me —
She was really so sweet
I could feel my heart beat
I'd have knelt at her feet (flourish, flourish,) *if she'd let me . . .*

Darkness fell. My mother unearthed a bottle of Green Goddess cocktail; we then polished off the remainder of the birthday cake and my school friends —in velour school hats and with moustaches in varying stages of disintegration — finally stumbled home hic-coughing away.

And the next day of course I discovered that my mother topped the Amazing Mothers League without the slightest difficulty. No one else's mother had a look in, not even the one who had allegedly met Mrs. Simpson coming out of the ladies' powder room at the Savoy three weeks before the Abdication.

'Your mother's absolutely spiffing!' they said. 'Why on earth did you make up all those ghastly lies about her?'

I told them I didn't know, because I didn't like to chance my arm by saying that I was practising to become a world famous author. Just at that moment, things were fine as they were.

20

But there's a darker side to mothers-and-daughters. Most of them travel over emotional rough patches at some time or another — what human relationship doesn't? — but in some cases what probably began as a casual spat develops into a lifetime of implacable hatred. Sometimes I think there's no hatred like it.

A famous example was that of Emerald Cunard and her daughter Nancy, who appeared to nurse an exquisite loathing for one another until death released them. Then there was the rough-tongued and over-worked Lancashire daughter who, in addition to a husband and five bawling children, had to contend with a hypochondriac mother who insisted on living with them.

'Eeh Maggie, Ah'm deeing — Ah'm deeing . . .'

'*Deeing?*' said Maggie bitterly. 'Tha'll na dee. They'll have fert shoot thee . . .'

On the other hand, it's not unusual for mother and daughter relationships to become close-knit to the point of claustrophobia. The Victorians were renowned for this, for at a time when masculine chauvinism and feminine fortitude had reached a kind of apogee, a lot of mothers found it comforting to lavish their tenderest affections on their daughters, and many a young woman's natural longings must have been gently murdered during the long afternoons of *petit point* with a mama who had found the whole business of Man and Marriage a bitter anti-climax in more senses than one.

> *Poor women! In this world of toil*
> *Keep up your hearts with prayer;*
> *Still trust in God and do your best —*
> *You never need despair,*

wrote Mary Sewell, an energetic and earnestly philanthropic Quaker burdened with an ineffectual husband.

She made a useful income from publishing her high-minded rum-te-rum verses, while pouring an endless flood of stifling affection upon her spinster daughter, who collapsed under the strain and became an invalid. Like Florence Nightingale and Elizabeth Barrett Browning, she took to the sofa, and while her mother sat close by writing *Homely Chats for the Working Man's Fireside*, daughter Anna quietly scribbled away at a minor masterpiece called *Black Beauty*. She dedicated it to her *dear and honoured Mother*, and died, as unobtrusively as she had lived, a few months after its publication.

But if the two Sewells present a first-class study in emotional suffocation, I feel sure that the prize for the most enigmatic relationship of all time must be awarded to Queen Anne Boleyn and her daughter Elizabeth Tudor.

It's true that there wasn't a lot of time for them to get acquainted — Anne was beheaded on Tower Hill when Elizabeth was only two years and eight months old — but even so they appear to have seen remarkably little of one another. In some degree it was due to the conventions of the time, but from Anne's point of view I think that any natural affection must have been soured by the bitter knowledge that she had made the awful mistake of having a girl instead of a boy. (And King Henry's first words to her at the conclusion of the second attempt, when hours of agony resulted in the delivery of a stillborn boy, are surely the most daunting of any father on record: 'I will speak to you, Madam, when you are well.')

There's plenty of evidence to suggest that Anne was arrogant, shallow, cruel and perhaps even a shade unbalanced, but oh Lord, it's a terrible thing to decapitate a woman merely because she doesn't give birth to the sort of baby you happen to need for the succession. But Henry was bored with her anyway, and with Jane Seymour already waiting in the wings, she was summoned before the Council and accused of multiple adultery. It seems generally assumed that she was innocent, but she had to go. And during the

23

five days she spent awaiting execution she spoke lovingly of her husband and her brother, but never once mentioned her daughter.

And throughout the seventy years of her own life Elizabeth was equally unforthcoming about her mother. Did she hate her? Despise her for her shrill instability, for her injudicious meddling in religious and political matters? On many occasions she spoke of her father with loving admiration — despite the fact that at one stage he had had her formally declared a bastard — but on the subject of her poor, haunted young mother, the voice of that most marvellously shrewd and witty woman is silent.

4

Mothers, and How to Treat Them

A lot of things that apply to animals also apply to *mater sapiens*, particularly during the early post-natal period, so whether she's a horse or a cat or a lady living in Ashton-under-Lyme, you won't go far wrong if you start by admiring her baby. Admire it, but make no attempt to handle it without first seeking her permission. Admirers who push their luck have been clawed by cats, bitten by horses and savaged verbally (if not physically) by the human species. It's a genuinely tricky time, too close to laughter and tears to be comfortable, so whatever your relationship to any particular mother and baby — be admiring, be affectionate, but remember to observe a decent self-restraint.

Some of the people who behave most rottenly to mothers, are babies. During the first weeks of life they seem to pursue a deliberate policy of Take All and Give Nowt, which can be very disconcerting for first-time mothers.

'Why does it just lie there snarling at me?' wept a frustrated young mother of my acquaintance, and although the nurse at the Welfare Clinic pointed out that it lay there because it was too young to get up, and that what passed for a snarl was merely a spasm of wind, she remained unconvinced and went on at great length about the Female Predicament and the Motherhood Trap until the day came when she picked the baby up and it smiled at her. It was a real intelligent smile of recognition that started in its eyes and spread to its hitherto thin and avaricious lips. They parted in an upward curve, displaying in the process a wide expanse of disarmingly naked gum, and the real relationship between mother and son, I'm glad to record (and I was there at the time), began from then on. He is now a highly paid expert on the International Monetary System and she is a merry grey-haired old lady who believes that the art of spreading happiness lies in the ability to tell fibs and who is also involved, so they tell me, in a movement to urbanise the snow leopard.

But if babies are mean to mothers, children under the age of seven or eight are invariably lavish in their affections and it takes a long period of calculated ill-treatment on mother's part before her offspring's natural feelings are finally done to death.

'I love my mother because she's big and pretty and goes sort of pink and shaky when I cuddle her,' confided one doting daughter of around five. To the uninvolved it may sound like snuggling up to a blancmange, but love like that is an essentially private business between two consenting people and if it's all right with them who am I to titter?

Right Reverend and Worshipful Mother, I recommend me unto your good Mothership, beseeching you to give me your daily benediction, desiring heartily to hear of your prosperity, which God preserve to his pleasure and to your heart's desire . . .

Thus wrote Oxford undergraduate Walter Paston to his mother Margaret. Hard to envisage them cuddling, but it was the thing to treat mothers with a high degree of respectful awe in 1478. Walter may even have laid it on a bit thicker than usual because he was hopefully enclosing the *whole sum of my expenses till Easter last past,* a sum which amounted to eight shillings. I hope she paid up and even tipped him a bit extra, because the poor boy died the following year.

Which brings me to wonder how much mother and child relationships are influenced by the prevailing mortality rate. If a woman produces an offspring every year, one of which dies every third year, it's bound to

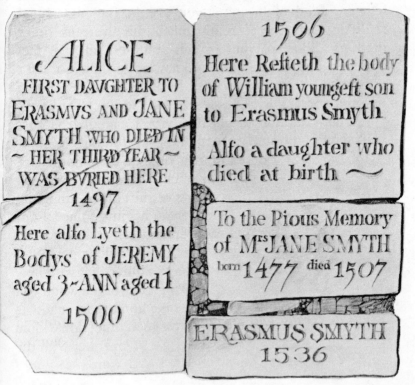

introduce a certain air of fatalism, of *déjà vu*, and one can imagine medieval mothers refusing to become too involved with any mewling little creature that has only a one-in-three chance of reaching maturity. On the other hand, the knowledge that she had probably only got her baby on a temporary basis may have had the effect of making her love it all the more. Perhaps to have sons and daughters still kicking about when they're sixty or seventy gets to be a bit of a drag; I don't know, mine haven't got there yet.

But to return to mothers and the treatment thereof: if you are between the ages of ten and fifteen it's highly probable that the early rapture of the relationship has dimmed a little, in your eyes at least. You may still be very fond of her, but you are in the process of realising that she is really much the same as other mothers. Some of your friends' mothers may in fact appear a better bet, and the knowledge that you can't swop her — there is no easy form of divorce between parents and children — merely adds to the frustration.

In this situation the best advice I can give is that you should attempt to explain your feelings to her.

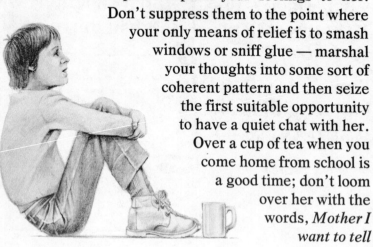

Don't suppress them to the point where your only means of relief is to smash windows or sniff glue — marshal your thoughts into some sort of coherent pattern and then seize the first suitable opportunity to have a quiet chat with her. Over a cup of tea when you come home from school is a good time; don't loom over her with the words, *Mother I want to tell*

you something awful while she's basting the roast or trying to scrub the mud out of your football shorts. Wait, as I say, for a suitable opportunity. In the average family they can occur at least two or three times a day, only you must learn to be nimble at spotting them.

So. You and your mother are alone and preferably sipping some kind of hot and comforting beverage, during which time you propose breaking the news to her that you find her inadequate. (Or bossy, or stupid, or square, whatever.)

Don't blurt it out immediately. Start gradually and work up to it. Begin by referring to all the wonderful moments you have shared in the past, like the Sports Day when she came first in the Mothers' Egg-and-Spoon Race and the time she cured your wart by spitting on it. Contrary to some opinions, I don't regard this as lulling her into a state of false security, so much as anaesthetising her before the shock, for in every surgical operation must come the moment when the scalpel makes contact with the tender skin. And this is when you, the surgeon, must make your incision in the poor woman's flesh quickly and concisely.

Tell her swiftly and without stumbling that you think she's foolish, or frivolous, or untrustworthy, or whatever it may be, and when you have done so, remember

29

our surgical analogy and repair the wound you have been forced to make as rapidly as possible. Stitch it up by telling her that you are convinced of her ability to recognise the error of her ways and that within a very short space of time all this unpleasantness will be a thing of the past; encourage her recovery by telling her that she can still make very nice puddings, and plan if possible a future treat — some sort of emotional convalescence, such as taking her to a double-bill horror movie or making her a balsa wood Messerschmitt for her dressing-table. Above all, show her that you still love her, because no woman on earth is prepared to go through all the fag of trying to mend her ways for someone who doesn't care two straws about her anyway.

If, however, you should find that she doesn't take too kindly to your home truths — in extreme cases she may even snap back with a few of her own — don't lose heart. It could be that, despite all your care you picked on the wrong moment, or that you are the owner of a mother with a particularly strong sense of self-righteousness. All you can do in either instance is to peg away gently and courteously, remembering that (i) Rome wasn't built in a day, and (ii) one practical example is worth ten verbal criticisms.

Thus, if your grouse is that she no longer runs round after you like she did when you were little — take her a cup of early morning tea. This will most likely astound and disarm her and may even cause an interesting little contretemps between her and your father, which of course is nothing to do with you. (It's nothing to do with me either, because fathers don't really come within the scope of this book.)

And finally, should yours be one of those rare cases when a seemingly endless period of pegging away with cups of tea and little home-truths, interspersed with offers to clean the brass, appears to bear no fruit — don't lose faith. I hate to say this, but it's just remotely possible that by the time you are sixteen or seventeen, you may suddenly discover that she's not so bad after all. Nothing to compare with Madame Curie or Rosa Luxembourg or course, but — well, just a little less abysmal than you'd thought.

But if children can suffer the bitter pangs of dis-enchantment, so can mothers.

He is not at all in good looks, moaned Queen Victoria in a letter referring to her eldest son. *His nose and mouth are too enormous and he pastes his hair down on his head and wears his clothes frightfully — he really is anything but good-looking . . . that coiffure really is too hideous with his small head and enormous features. He is grown, however . . .*

Poor Bertie. He and his mother never did manage to see eye to eye, but I think a sort of weary tolerance finally set in, he rising above her endless fussing and fidgeting, while she did her best to ignore his amatory escapades.

Sometimes though, the mother-and-son relationship works so well that it's far cosier than any marriage; it can even outstrip the Sewell syndrome when it comes to creating that particular brand of sweet and soggy devotion. In many instances, the situation is brought about by early widowhood on mother's part and by a marked reluctance to discover what makes other women tick on the part of her son. So far as he's concerned it's a matter of allowing familiarity to breed content.

I know an interesting story about one such couple. Their name was Ellenbogen and they lived lovingly in a neat house with standard roses and a chiming doorbell, and on the writing desk in the window stood a photograph of poor Dadda, a civil engineer who had perished in an earthquake in Venezuela. It had happened over forty years ago, when little Marty was only three, and although his memories of Dadda had become pretty blurred, he retained a respectful affection for the square face with its watchful eyes and resolute jaw. As for Mother, she was a tiny woman with a tittuppy walk and a little sharp nose stuck between two carefully rouged cheeks, and she ran the home with competence while maintaining the air of a sweet invalid.

'Poor Mother feels the cold quite pitifully,' Marty would say, as he arranged her mohair shawl with his big kind hands.

'I always think,' Mother would say as she sank daintily within its folds, 'that no daughter can ever be as sensitive as a sensitive son.'

One summer evening when Mother was resting and Marty was setting off for a stroll, he saw an old man leaning on the front gate. He shifted to one side as Marty approached and said 'Good-evening, Mr. Ellenbogen.'

'Good-evening,' said Marty, then paused. 'How did you know my name?'

The old man smiled. He wore a greasy homberg and a torn raincoat that drooped below his knees. Dirt lined the creases of his face and he had a mildewed smell.

'Ah-ha.'

'If it's money you want,' said Marty primly, 'I don't give to casual strangers.'

He began to walk away. Behind him he heard the soft flip-flap of broken shoes.

'I want to tell you something, Mr. Ellenbogen.'

'There's nothing I want to hear,' said Marty. 'So be off.'

Oh, Mr. Ellen*bogen*,' said the old man breathing

mildew on the back of Marty's neck. 'There's some-thing it's really time I told you.'

Conscious that people were staring, Marty halted. He looked with distaste at the dirty face and leering smile.

'Well?'

'I'm your dad.'

Marty recoiled. Then laughed.

'Listen, my son. You were born on the 11th of July in 1935 and christened Martin Makepeace Ellenbogen and you had your tonsils out when you were five. You Mum's name is Winifred Grace and she's got a funny little horseshoe scar on her how-d'you-do.'

'But — how . . .?'

'I dunno. She came by it before we got acquainted.'

'Clear off!' cried Marty in a sudden shrill voice. 'You're a maniac! —'

'I know it's come as a shock, son —'

'It so happens that my father was Victor Makepeace Ellenbogen, who died in 1938 and is still mourned by my mother and myself,' Marty said a little more calmly. 'He was a civil engineer and a gentleman and any comparison between the two of you is too ludicrous to contemplate. So clear off.' He marched away.

'Down the road on the left there's a pub,' said the tramp, breathing down the back of his neck once more. 'I'll meet you in there in half an hour and you'll have all the ready cash you can lay hands on. If you don't, I'll start taking steps to correct some of the family facts you seem to have got so wrong.'

'Dadda is *dead*! —' cried Marty involuntarily.

'That's what she's brought you up to believe,' said the tramp. 'See you in half an hour — son.'

It was insane. It was unthinkable. Tiptoing rapidly past the sofa where Mother lay resting, Marty picked up Dadda's photograph and examined it carefully. Then relaxed. The resolute jaw and watchful eyes bore no likeness whatever to the tramp who had accosted him. And yet . . . Marty peered closer, and agitation returned when he fancied that there was something about the mouth, and maybe something about the cut of the nostrils . . .

'What are you doing with darling Dadda?' asked a plaintive little voice from within the mohair shawl.

'Mother dear,' said Marty, 'did you actually *go* to Dadda's funeral?'

'To Venezuela? How could I?'

'Do you know if anyone saw him when he was dead? I mean, supposing he'd only been stunned by falling masonry and had lost his memory —'

'Dearest,' said Mother, 'I have been receiving a Company pension for over forty years, have I not?'

Marty mumbled agreement, and headed for the door.

Unaccustomed to pubs, he stood uncertainly on the threshold. Smart local people were chatting together round the bar and at a lone table in the corner sat the tramp. He was drinking half a bitter and he smiled when he saw Marty.

'Don't take my generosity for any kind of admission regarding our relationship,' said Marty, taking out his wallet. 'I certainly don't believe you, but if by any chance you are . . . you *are* . . . well, all I can say is that you've left it far too late.' He laid four five pound notes on the table.

'Jesus, how I loved that little horseshoe scar,' said the tramp, dreamily pocketing the notes.

Once again Marty forced himself to study the old man's features. Beneath the dirt and the smell of mildew, the strange and terrible familiarity of the mouth and nostrils filled him with a squeamish horror.

He looked at the coarse old hand with its broken nails and shuddered to imagine it guiding poor dear little Mother down the aisle as a bride. Jealouse rage filled him, making his eyes protrude.

'Get out! —' he cried. 'Get out of our lives, you verminous old deadbeat! After all these years I've no more use for a father than Mother has for a husband —'

The tramp flinched, as if he had received a blow. Slowly he drained his glass, wiped his mouth on his cuff and stood up. He began to flip-flap away in his broken shoes, then paused. He came back again.

'*Husband*?' he said gently. 'Listen, my son, who said anything about me being your Mum's husband?'

And in a Chapter entitled Mothers and How to Treat Them, I'm not quite sure where that leaves us. Let's just settle for loving the positive and being charitable enough to gloss over the odd little bit of negative, should we ever have reason to suspect it.

3

A Short Dissertation on Mothers-in-Law

ne of the nastiest plants I know is the *Sansevieria trifasciata laurentii*. It has long, thin, stiff leaves with dangerously serrated edges, and any attempt to cheer itself up by varying its dingy workhouse green with the odd stripe of yellow or grey, works not at all. It's a waste of time. It's a morose plant, a lugubrious plant, and it takes the analytical eye of the trained horticulturalist to tell whether it's actually alive or dead. The Dutch adore it. And so do the Belgians.

A few years ago I spent a lot of time traipsing round Belgium in the cold and wet, gathering material about civilian life during the First World War, and every octogenarian that I interviewed had one proudly on view in the window. I thought of it as an Old Person's Plant; the sort of plant that debilitated old ladies like to fondle with a feather duster. Then I discovered that everyone over there has one in their window, that it's a sort of Low Countries' Categorical Imperative. Hotels, and those of a particularly ebullient nature, finish off the effect by tying a bright red ribbon round either the pot or the lower extremities of the plant itself. The effect is macabre, and always takes me back to the days of my childhood when people used to bind a scarlet ribbon round their sleeve to indicate that they had been vaccinated.

I do not like the *Sansevieria trifasciata laurentii* and resent even more the fact that its nickname is Mother-in-Law's Tongue.

Still, one has to admit that mothers-in-law have received an almost unrelievedly bad press ever since the Middle Ages. *This gaudy Piece, this strutting scold, this wither'd hag with viper's breath* . . . exclaimed one Humphry de Cuvier of his wife's mother, and it's gone on like that until the present day. Or certainly until the demise of the Music Hall, and Max Miller in particular.

Why was this? If humour is supposed to be a method of transforming the fearful into the merely ridiculous, why were men so frightened of the women who had mothered their wives? I recently consulted a long-married American academic on this point: *I only come up to her shoulder*, he said. And speaking of academics, how about Bertrand Russell's statement that *Mothers-in-law are a very stubborn part of the Mystery of Evil*. It makes you feel that we're only a stone's throw away from blood sacrifice.

But if mothers-in-law were universally horrendous — and I'm certainly not admitting that they were, mind — perhaps it was because up until very recently women have always had to substitute influence for authority. Reading history, it's astonishing how often a man's career has been furthered by the flutter of his wife's eyelashes in the right direction — not necessarily a case of she was laid and he was made, but the art of diplomacy comes easily to women and it must often have been maddening not to be allowed to practise it in a more recognisedly official capacity. As it was, they had to confine their skills to the family circle, and by the time their children were of marriageable age, were extremely adept at the smiling snub and the sweetly worded put-down. (And don't forget, incidentally, that the young-and-in-love are among the most pitifully vulnerable creatures in the world. Like earthworms, it takes only the slightest pressure to squash them flat.)

Alternatively, ill-behaved mothers-in-law could well have been caused by a combination of jealousy and the menopause bitterly proclaiming a final and inescapable farewell to youth. Even in these days, few women can behold a starry-eyed daughter at the chancel steps without making a fleeting comparison between the comely young bridegroom and the portly and bespectacled Old Familiar who's doing the giving away. She still loves him, but suddenly all she can see ahead is fireside slippers and an Over-Sixties coachtrip to Clacton. It gives her a morbid feeling.

It was a great pity the way the menopause used to coincide with the acquisition of in-law children, particularly in the days when the greater a subject's importance, the less chance there was of discussing it, and many a no more than mildly irritated mother-in-law must have been seen as crimson with fury merely because delicacy forbade her to explain that she was having a hot flush.

Hot flushes, spare tyres, sick headaches, searing doubts and scalding discontents. Questions like *What does it all mean?* and *Where are we all going?* rising up like spectres in the dead of night, together with cramp in the calf muscles and a sudden mad desire for the man next door. The more it was all suppressed, the worse it became, and whispered stories about the

county asylum being stuffed full of raving middle-aged women did nothing to help. If you half-expect to go insane, the chances are that you will.

'Don't mind Mother,' the family would say, grimacing, 'she's at a funny age.'

The precise age, in other words, at which they proposed to introduce her to a brand new, grown-up child, confident in the expectation that she would immediately clutch it to her bosom with a glad cry.

But it takes time. Most mothers (menopausal or not) are capable of swift sympathy, and have an instinct to open their arms to any young stray creature, but the majority of potential in-law children already have a good home. And a loving mother. And when you remember that most of us used to stand on ceremony much more (*Mother dear, this is Mr. Smith. Frederick dear, this is my mother, Mrs. Brown . . .*) it's not surprising that a lot of young people, already brainwashed by Music Hall jokes, had their worst suspicions instantly confirmed by the initial meeting with this strained, simmering woman with creaking corsets and a face like a turbulent sunset.

But it's all marvellously different now. For one thing, a lot of mothers have careers outside the home, and the latest candidate for mother-in-lawdom may well be too engrossed in preparing a report on Population Dynamics to do more than flip a cheerful hand in the appropriate direction. She's too busy even to be jealous. And for another thing, the menopause, like the ducking-stool, is a thing of the past. Young women are no longer brought up in the expectation of being put away for a couple of years in their forties, and a course of hormone replacement therapy puts paid to hot flushes.

41

Today's mother-in-law is a younger, livelier woman, who bounds about in a Playtex bra and pastel-coloured curls, but should any son-in-law absentmindedly mistake her for her daughter, Old Familiar will no doubt still be there to remind him quietly of his error.

5
How to be a
Good Grandmother

ccording to the Guinness Book of Records, it's theoretically possible to have great-great-great-great-grandparents all alive, alive-O, but great-great-great-grandparents are about as much as you're likely to get. It's not just a question of keeping old folk alive longer, you've also got to extend the period during which women are capable of breeding. To which I personally am opposed. Up to the age of eighteen, women should be acquiring an education; after the age of forty they should be free to put their feet up and read a book for an hour or two. And having hurled that challenging statement, let's get back to grandmothers.

It's interesting how the idea of becoming a grandmother invariably brings with it an element of shock. Time and again, mature and intelligent mothers of nubile young women have become struck all of a heap by the news that their little girls are preggers. And I suppose that's it; few mothers see their children as adults — at least not completely, and not all the time. They've only got to be ill or unhappy and the poor old maternal fingers begin itching to soothe away the pain, even if it means standing on a box to do so. And to all but the most incurably matter-of-fact, the first sight of a daughter who has just had her first pregnancy confirmed, brings a lump to the throat, a mist before the eyes and an uncontrollable urge to start knitting.

I only wish I could go through it for you dear, and save you all the annoyance, wrote Queen Victoria to her daughter, the Crown Princess of Prussia. And most mothers will sympathise with the Royal instinct to enfold and protect. I once knew a woman, by the way, who put on seven inches round the waist while her daughter, who was pregnant, increased by only five. As soon as the baby was born, both returned to their normal measurements with a sigh of gratification.

And if it comes as a curious sort of shock to be told that you're about to become a grandmother, you receive an additional jolt when the thing becomes a *fait accompli*. I don't believe I've met a woman yet who wasn't rendered incoherent for a moment or two by the first sight of her daughter sitting up in bed and saying, 'Oh, it was nothing, really.' (When I speak of daughters, incidentally, it must be assumed to include daughters-in-law, because by this time there should be virtually no difference between the two. They all need loving, and they all *belong*, and if it wasn't for them there would be no grandmothers anyway.)

I don't know whether anyone has ever done an economic survey on grandmothers, but if they did, I bet they'd be surprised by the amount of money they've saved their families. In all parts of the world for many centuries past, people who work for their living have found it useful, if not essential, to dust old Granny down and bring her back into circulation with the birth of each new child, so that she can look after it while its mother resumes the task of working to earn cash. And to the women who spent sixteen hours a day in the mines or in the cotton mills, I suppose the task of washing and cooking for half a dozen children was considered a light job, suitable for a retired person.

In higher circles, grandmothers often did the same thing, but for different reasons, and history is full of dreadful, despotic old women who brushed their daughters-in-law aside and took over the entire management of their children. Catherine the Great wasn't even allowed to see hers.

I know I've spent a lot of time in this book extolling the marvels of mothers, but I have to admit that when the maternal instinct gets out of hand — or when, in the case of grandmothers, it won't lie down — the situation can become very ugly. It's easy to understand that Granny has spent fifty years garnering practical experience of the utmost value and that all she wants to do is to give it to you freely and without let or hindrance, because she sometimes gets this chill little feeling that she won't be here for ever and ever, and that when she's gone it will all just float away and dissipate itself into the ether, or wherever it is that experience goes to after we're dead — but alas, the average human being is only capable of assimilating good advice in very small quantities. It would far sooner find out for itself. And the fact that a lot of the advice most determinedly inflicted is often of an undeniably trivial nature, merely adds a final touch of hysteria to the whole wretched business.

As it happens, I recently conducted a small survey of my own, concerning the putting on and securing of babies' napkins during the past sixty years, and the results were fascinating indeed.

Basically there are only two different methods of applying napkin to baby, that is supposing you are equipped with the classic square of material like a large towelling handkerchief. (My own daughter-in-law uses things that look like a filleted plaice, but then she's French, and her rather *outré* objects are beyond the scope of this particular study.)

But to return to the more familiar towelling square, one method of approach is to fold it into a triangle and pin it in the middle, and the other is to fold it into an oblong and secure it with a pin down either side. The main reason given for discarding the Triangle in favour of the Oblong every now and then, is that it makes the baby bandy, and then the Oblong is in turn rejected on the grounds that it doesn't absorb so much of the wet. (Very occasionally mothers have to abandon the Oblong for the Triangle, merely because they have lost one of the two pins required, but that is neither here not there.)

Most young and inexperienced mothers are naturally anxious to follow the method currently advocated by the baby experts — not to do so is social death at the Welfare Clinic — and careful research has proved quite conclusively that the Triangle and the Oblong alternate in popularity about once in every ten years. Thus:

EXPERT'S ADVICE

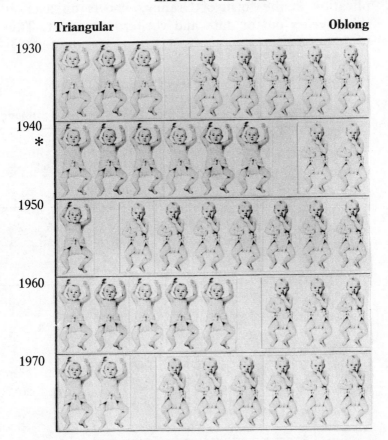

* Towards the end of 1944 there was a period when babies had
no pins at all, because they had all been requisitioned to make
Wellington bombers. (The pins, not the babies.)

All well and good, but here comes a needless complication in the form of Granny, who is on average thirty years out of date and vociferous with it. Thus we have:

GRANNY'S ADVICE

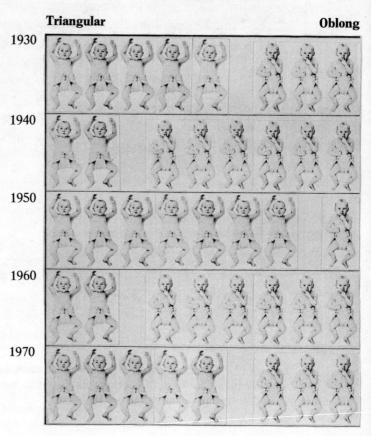

From which it will instantly be seen that all grandmothers find themselves in direct opposition to everyone else when it comes to babies' napkins, and no one would believe the running battles, the grim-lipped feuds and the secret skirmishes at dead of night that lie behind these two seemingly innocuous graphs. Catholic versus Protestant pales into insignificance by comparison with side-pinners and centre-pinners.

All I can advise is this: if you are the baby's mother — be patient. All women, whether they have given birth or not, begin to lose a little of their mental elasticity by the time they are forty-five. By the time they are fifty, they have become dyed in the wool, and anywhere between the ages of fifty-five and sixty they start repeating themselves. But this doesn't stop them from being kind, and loving, and eager to do their best — and anyway, this particular argument shouldn't be of long duration, because all babies should be finished with napkins by the age of eighteen months.

Therefore, if you're a grandmother, my advice to you is stay out of the scene until you're invited. The advent of a baby in the family after twenty years of being without one, goes to some women's heads like wine, but you must remember that you, as Granny, must take a back seat. You've had your turn. This may sound harsh, but it's a well-known fact that

She who shoved
Was never loved.

And anyway, prolonged ill-feeling can shorten people's lives.

Once upon a time a little girl called Red Riding Hood went tripping through the forest with a basket of convenience foods on her arm. She was going to visit her grandmother, who lived in a charming little cottage *orné*, up to its thatch in roses and clematis.

Grandmother was a brisk and smiling old lady who didn't look a day past sixty.

'Come in, my dear, come in,' she said, taking Red Riding Hood's arm. 'It's too late for elevenses, so we'll have a little drop of something else.' And she went to the cupboard for the dry sherry and biscuits.

Red Riding Hood removed her cloak, and while her grandmother poured the sherry, she unpacked the basket, then they both sat down.

'Chin-chin!' said Red Riding Hood.

'Bottoms up!' replied her grandmother.

They exchanged news, and when it became apparent (as it always did) that, by virtue of living in the village, Red Riding Hood had far more news than poor Grandmother, who lived in the middle of the forest — the child asked the old lady whether she didn't feel lonely and out of things.

'Heavens no,' said Grandmother. 'At my age one is more than content to sit back and contemplate the vagaries of others.'

Red Riding Hood said, perhaps a little contemptuously (for she was but a child after all), that she wouldn't have thought there was much opportunity for studying people's vagaries, or anything else, living where she did. Grandmother smiled. And then poured a little more sherry.

They went on to discuss the iniquitous price of fish, then suddenly Red Riding Hood sneezed. And then discovered that she had lost her handkerchief.

'Borrow one of mine,' said Grandmother. 'Top left hand drawer in my dressing-table.'

'Thank you, Grandmother dear,' said Red Riding Hood, and went upstairs to the bedroom. Fifteen seconds later she was back, white as paper.

'Grandmother —' she said, 'Oh Grandmother — I

don't know how to tell you this, but there's an
enormous wolf sitting up in your bed wearing your
nightie!'

'Yes, I know,' said Grandmother. 'He's a trans-
vestite.'

'But this is terrible —' cried Red Riding Hood.
'He might eat you!'

'No chance,' replied Grandmother. 'I'm far too
tough, and anyway he's a tinned dog food freak.'

'Even so,' cried Red Riding Hood, still greatly distressed, 'you can't just let strange wolves in, and have them sitting up in your bed wearing your clothes — he's probably got fleas, and besides, what would people think?'

'My poor child, you are quite distraught,' said Grandmother soothingly. 'Now blow your nose and attend to me.'

Red Riding Hood did so. They both sipped a little more sherry.

'The first thing to bear in mind,' went on Grandmother, 'is that wolves are a threatened species. There are very few of them left, and it is up to us to do all within our power to conserve them.'

'But in zoos, surely,' muttered Red Riding Hood.

'Zoos are the obvious choice, but what's wrong with the forest where they belong? And if one particular member of this poor beleagured tribe should derive some sort of harmless kick from wearing my nightie for a couple of hours a week — he's most punctilious about only borrowing it during the day, despite the fact that wolves are naturally nocturnal in their habits — who am I to say nay? As for fleas, I've never been particularly bothered by them yet, but in any case why is the bite of a flea so much more shameful than the bite of a mosquito? They are all God's creatures. And as for what people think — my dear child, I have lived for almost a hundred years, and if during the course of that time I have learned to regard those about me with a certain degree of tolerance, affection and humour, surely that is not to be condemned?'

Red Riding Hood blew her nose again and said, Well no, perhaps it wasn't. She had never thought of it like that before.

'Of course you haven't. Before the age of twenty,

one invariably confuses feeling with thinking.'

'But wearing your *nightie* —'

'Oh come now, it's merely a question of what turns you on,' said Grandmother, then raised benevolent eyes to the ceiling as they heard a couple of soft thuds overhead. 'So now my child, go to the cupboard and fetch another glass because I believe our friend is coming down to join us.'

The wolf bounded into the room in a flurry of white nightie, and when he saw Red Riding Hood he smiled and shook her by the hand. Then Grandmother poured some more sherry and proposed a toast to Imperturbability, and after that they danced and sang and told jokes and had a perfectly marvellous time until Red Riding Hood, flushed and happy, suddenly realised that she should have been home hours ago.

'Where on earth have you been all this time?' demanded her mother and father. 'We were so worried, we thought you must have met a wolf!'

'I did,' said Red Riding Hood, but when she tried to tell them about it, they became very angry and called her an anthropomorphist, and as if that wasn't enough, they sent the poor little thing away to a College of Further Education to find out what it meant. And by the time she came home again, Grandmother had died and the wolf had been shot, stuffed, and placed in a museum. Which is sad in a way, but inevitable.

Old age is inevitable too, but there's no reason why it should be sad. Nature is in many ways kinder than we think — why do we grow short-sighted if it isn't to spare us the vexation of seeing all the wrinkles? — and I often feel thankful for the way in which the human memory seems to pursue a deliberate policy of emphasising the best and discarding the worst.

Whenever I allow my thoughts to amble back to my schooldays, they invariably appear bathed in summer light, with smiling chums and benign mistresses and mathematics that I understood, whereas one or two faded snaps and a couple of blotty exercise books have survived to tell a very different tale; the chums in the snaps look as if they would like to poison me and the exercise books speak of an embryonic writer already steaming to produce fine literature which no one is going to want. *You must not write so dramatically!* cried a desperate history mistress in red ink. *I asked for an impartial opinion of Mary Queen of Scots and you have written a third-rate thriller. See me after the lesson.*

I wonder where she is now. And whether she too is a grandmother.

Which reminds me, for some reason, of the under-graduate who took a breakfast tray to his aged and much loved grandmother's room one morning and found her sitting up in bed reading the bible. Surprised, he asked the reason.

'I'm swotting for my finals,' she said.

Old age is a time of letting go. Of shrugging off the hassle and the heartache, of folding the hands in the lap and dozing while someone else gets tea ready. It's a time for not caring what you look like so long as you're warm, and a time for telling authority to go to hell.

And if you never dared to love wholeheartedly when you were young, you can do so now with impunity. No one's going to laugh, or search for ulterior motives, because they instinctively recognise that the love of an old person is quiet and undemanding; attaching

strings takes time, and time is the one commodity they're short of.

Old age is when you sit back and watch all the fragments fall into place; when people from the past float back into your mind and the person you're actually talking to floats out of it. And it doesn't matter. They make allowances. Old age means forgetting where you put things, and not worrying because experience has taught you that they'll turn up again sooner or later. Everything turns up again sooner or later, and old age sees to it that the less time there is in hand, the less need for any hurry.

Grandmother, Great-grandmother, Great-great-grandmother . . . You know you're one of them, but can't always remember which. There's a bald man with tired lines on his face who may be your son; a grey-haired woman in bifocals whom you suspect was once the little daughter who won a prize for toe-dancing. Now she helps you into bed every night and asks if your bowels are regular.

And then all the children. Some of them lanky and spotty and some of them still crawling. The lanky ones try to talk to you about Brecht and the Berliner Ensemble, and the little ones try to pull themselves up by the arm of your chair. You love them all and feel pleasantly aware that they're all here because of you, but you don't give a tinker's for Bertold Brecht, or how the baby's napkin is put on. These things don't matter any more. They've faded into the distance, and you know that ultimately everything ends in sleep.

Old age can also mean an old folks' home. Cream walls, cretonne curtains and nurses in little paper caps. One of whom will help you into bed and ask if your bowels are regular. Other grandmothers (Great? Great-great?) will pass you in the corridor, shuffling slowly in their Pirelli slippers, and out of the deepening twilight appears the bald man with the tired lines on his face. He has brought you a box of chocolates, and a passing therapist says: 'How lovely, dear! Ask nurse to give you your teeth . . .' (*Teeth? What teeth?*)

56

But it doesn't matter. Nothing matters. There are pills to soothe away pain and when death comes it means no more than closing a book. It wasn't a bad book on the whole and everything worked out right in the end. And you know that tomorrow someone will remember to cancel your library ticket for you.

A grandchild, maybe.

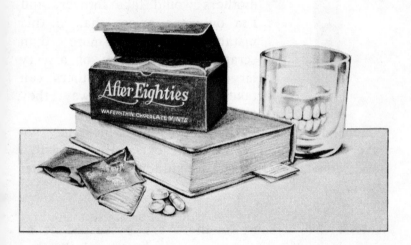

6

Mothers' Alphabet

o write the definitive book about mothers would take forever, and I'm only too aware that in this instance I've no more than scratched the surface of a very large subject, (and mothers can take that whichever way they choose).

Here, therefore, is a list of items which may not have been covered in the main text and which will, I hope, encourage the serious student towards further study.

AMBITION   Some mothers are possessed of an ambition for their young which can only be described as vaulting. The mothers themselves are generally rather stout, with square chins and a vigilant stare, while the young are almost unfailingly small and meek. To see these mothers at their best, one is advised to visit Competitive Festivals of Dance, Music, Drama etc. of which any number occur regularly throughout the country. Admission is generally free, but take sandwiches. Senior mothers in this category are also known to cluster thickly at any theatrical audition held for juvenile persons; Noel Coward once met a real beauty called Mrs. Worthington.

BOSOM   As practical use of the female bosom declines, so its importance as an object of contemplation appears to increase; despite its subjection to the ubiquitous feeding bottle and teat, it's been photographed far, far more than the Royal Family. Mothers' bosoms are still very good for crying on however, or for cushioning the head during the course of a short nap. Anatole France must have napped a lot because it was he who said that a woman with no bosom is like a bed without a pillow.

CONTRACEPTION   Mother-stopping.

DELIVERY   The moment when the baby shoots forth from its mother, and there ought to be a law that the people waiting outside to catch it should first warm their hands.

EMBRYO   is the human organism at an early stage of growth; at less than a week old it already has three distinct layers of cells. As development proceeds, it becomes known as a foetus, a strange, frowning little creature with a big head and fishy eyes. It's said that far more males are conceived than females, but they're not so good at staying the course. By the fourth month of pregnancy there are likely to be two male stillbirths (drop-outs?) for every one female, but on the whole we end up roughly even.

FOREBODING   Some mothers are very prone to this, and in a way it's like Ambition in reverse. Pregnant women can become convinced that they are about to give birth to anything other than a human baby, and even when it's born they can't bring themselves to believe that it will ever grow up to be of any practical use to anyone. These are generally mothers who have had a bad start in life, i.e. the ones who have never been told that they are clever or beautiful or important.

On the other hand, I wonder whether Hitler's mother felt a slight tremor of disquiet when she first clasped the new-born Adolph to her breast? God knows, she should have done.

GODMOTHERS, INCLUDING FAIRY   Human ones are generally your mother's best friend at the time of the christening, but by the time you're about ten and anxious to know what the Holy Ghost looks like, she's moved to another district and forgotten that you ever existed. Fairy ones only appear in pantomimes; they wear a lot of tinsel and are rather mealy-mouthed. Well, imagine going to all that trouble to get Cinderella to the ball and then expecting her to be home by midnight.

HYSTERECTOMY or Having the Whole Lot Out   This really means the removal of the reproductive organs and is often done because of fibroids growing in the uterus. A very standard operation nowadays (they have you back on your feet within twenty-four hours), but when my Auntie Minnie had it done back in 1927 they warned her that she might grow a beard and start chasing young girls. (She didn't, but the idea worried her no end.)

IMMACULATE CONCEPTION   Strictly the Virgin Mary's territory this, although down the ages lots of mothers-to-be, in varying stages of desperation, have tried it on as well. Generally without success.

JACK-IN-THE-CELLAR   18th Century slang for an unborn child.

KINDERGARTEN   Meaning literally children's garden. The idea was started in Germany by Friederich Froebel (1782-1852) as a friendly place where children of pre-school age could be gently broken in to the idea that Being Educated is Good.

LABOUR   The process by which the pregnant woman's muscles contract to expel the baby from her body. Also the name of a political party founded in 1900.

MOTHER   There is another sort, and it's the unpleasant gluey stuff which (and I quote) forms on the surface of a liquor undergoing acetous fermentation, consisting of the bacteria which are causing the fermentation. In other words, it's what you need for making vinegar.

NERVOUS SYSTEM   All living creatures have one, except I believe the sponge, and some people would claim that the nervous system of the human mother is about the most efficient and highly tuned in the world. It needs to be. Mothers' nervous systems enable them to hear a muffled hiccough at 30 paces at dead of night, to sense when illness is real and not sham, and also help them to deal with

juvenile rages, sulks, accidents and refusals to eat stewed rhubarb.

Subjecting such a complex mechanism to constant stress naturally results every now and then in temporary breakdown, a condition recognised with awe by even the layman. Symptoms are various and nearly all of them spectacular. The mother may weep copiously and declare that she *cannot go on*, or she may be discovered crouching in a corner with parched lips and wild eyes. She may become violent, particularly towards those closest to her, and in extreme cases may even rush out of the house and head for the river. On average, only the good swimmers plunge in.

Mothers suffering from this condition must be treated with firmness, with kindness, and above all with tact. They must be removed from the river, dried thoroughly and given a hot drink. They must be allowed to cry (preferably upon the father's shoulder), all children having meanwhile been banished from the room, and they must then be placed in a warm bed with the curtains drawn and perhaps a little soft music playing, and left to sleep for at least twelve hours.

Those crouching in corners must be persuaded out of them; this may take hours of patient cajolery, (one father I knew was only able to entice the mother from the cupboard under the stairs by offering to put all the children in a Home and then get a job in another town so that he only returned for a cooked meal once a week). Mothers suffering from prolonged bouts of weeping must have their tears dried with a soft handkerchief — there is something a little cursory about paper tissues — and they must be told in a quiet loving voice that there is no *need* for them to go on. No need at all. The whole place can fall apart and no one will give a damn so long as they'll comb their hair, powder their noses and stop trailing round in odd shoes. They used to be so beautiful, and they can be beautiful *again*, if only they'll smile, etc. etc.

And in every case, once a semblance of calm has been restored and the mother is once again able to contemplate her children without undue distress, (cunning fathers re-introduce them to her one by one), it is an excellent plan to live off the deep freeze for a week and blow all the house-keeping on something happy and wonderful and totally impractical, like a weekend in Paris, or six lessons in hang-gliding. Whatever you do, don't buy her anything for the kitchen.

OPTIMISM   As expressed by a lady called Aline Kilmer:
> *When people enquire I always just state*
> *I have four nice children and hope to have eight.*

PERAMBULATOR   A four-wheel vehicle used for conveying babies and very small children. In my day these were high and bouncy and had big wheels and graceful shallow bodies. They could be very snob. The modern ones are small, hard, flat and folding, and I suppose that the snob thing nowadays depends on the type of car it's loaded in to. Who cares if it looks like a plastic seed tray if it's rightful place is on the back seat of an Alfa Romeo?

QUEEN MOTHER   The consort of a deceased king and the mother of the reigning monarch, and as a breed becoming scarcer then hens' teeth.

RELAXATION   The thing you learn to do while you're pregnant so that when you give birth it doesn't hurt so much. Most mothers find that it helps, and those who forget how to do it when the drama is actually upon them tend to be glad they went to relaxation classes because they made some nice friends there.

STEP-MOTHERS   have an even worse reputation to bear than mothers-in-law, and I suspect that this is due in some measure to Hans Anderson and the Brothers Grimm.

Be a step-mother kindly as she will
There's in her love some hint of winter's chill . . .
wrote D'Arcy W. Thompson and maybe there's a hint of personal suffering in his words. I once knew a man of somewhat restless disposition, who by an almost unbelievably circuitous route took for his fifth wife the head prefect of his daughter's school. The prefect, an icy little number, exploited the situation by giving the junior girl stacks of impositions and 'lines', but the junior got her own back by shrilling 'Bravo, *Mummy*! —' when the head prefect went up to collect her four A-level certificates on Prize Day. Somehow they never became friends.

TETHYS   was a much more equable woman, and the greatest of the Greek sea deities. Her husband was Oceanus and she gave birth to all the main rivers of the universe, as well as a lot of daughters, known collectively as the Oceanides.

UTERUS, VAGINA, WOMB   We might as well take the next three together as they are all part

65

of a mother's vital equipment. Uterus and womb are one and the same thing, being the hollow container suspended within the pelvis in which the fertilized egg develops into a baby during the months of pregnancy.

A vacant womb is only about 3 inches long, but it can have stretched to over 12 by the time its occupant is due to leave. The lower end of the uterus (the cervix) projects down into the vagina, which is the muscular tube (on average about 4 inches long), down which the baby must travel before it sees the light of day. Upon arrival some babies have intimated that it seemed more like 4 miles.

XENOPHOBIA   is a nervous disorder from which some mothers can suffer and it manifests itself in a fear of strangers and/or anything known to be foreign. It can make holidays abroad an impossibility, and not all that long ago I met a poor woman tormented beyond endurance because all the children's clothes she attempted to buy were made in Hong Kong.

YETH-HOUNDS   According to West Country superstition these are headless dogs who are possessed by the spirits of children who have not been baptised. They wander over the moors at night making piteous wailing sounds.

ZYGOTE   The result of the union of two cells. Which is really where it all starts, and I think that this is perhaps a good time to say something about fathers.

Personally I'm very pro them. I've never met a

child yet who wasn't the better for having a mother and a father (preferably the same ones all the time), and I do hope that we're never, never going to be so foolish as to allow technology to diddle fathers out of the pleasant job of making women into mothers. I also think that fathers today are much nicer than they have ever been before; they wear vivid colours and varied hairstyles and no longer does the dark dread of effeminancy prevent them from cuddling babies or playing hopscotch on the hall floor if they feel so inclined.

In their own quiet way they too have become liberated, and despite the current passion for rasping on about social disintegration, I can't help feeling in my better moments that fathers, like mothers, are going to be with us for quite a long while yet.

Let's drink to that.